This is my pet.

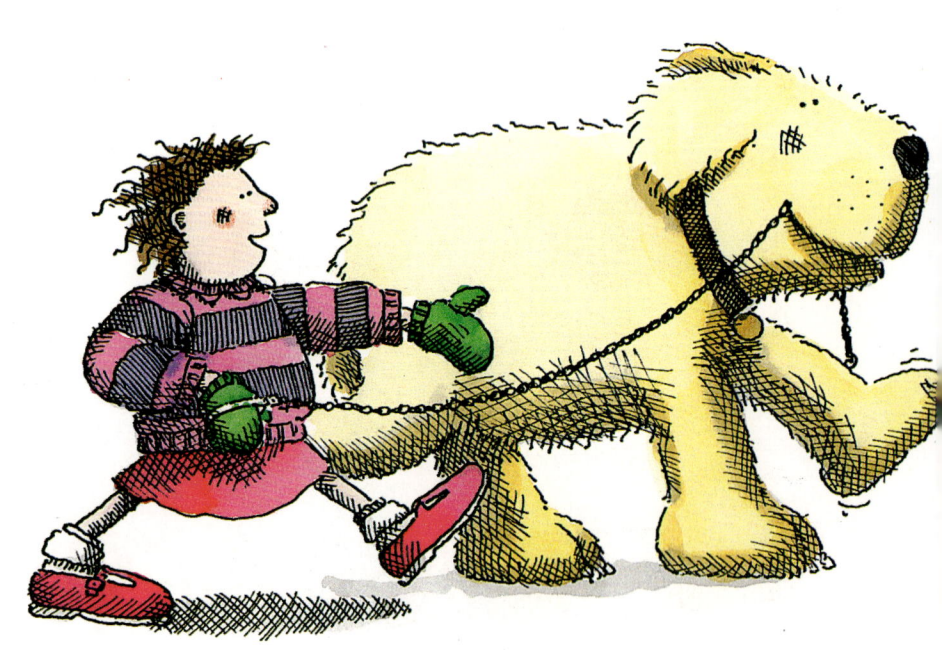

Sometimes I take her for a walk.

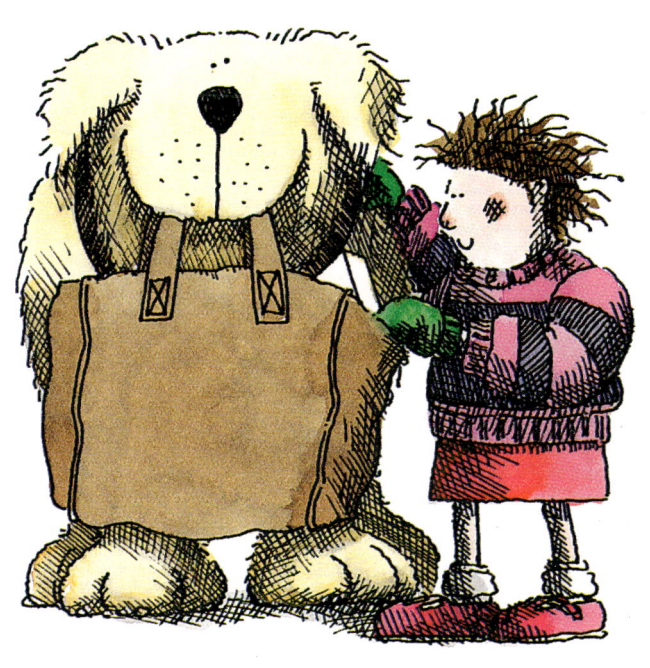

Sometimes I take her shopping.

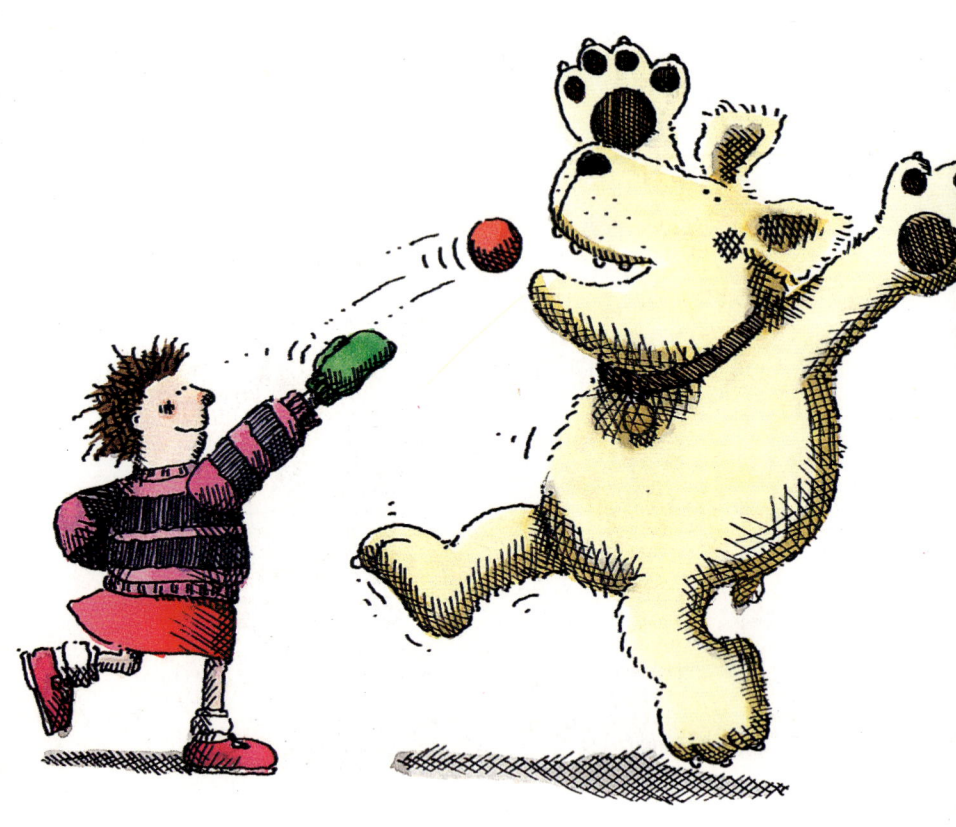

Sometimes I play with her.

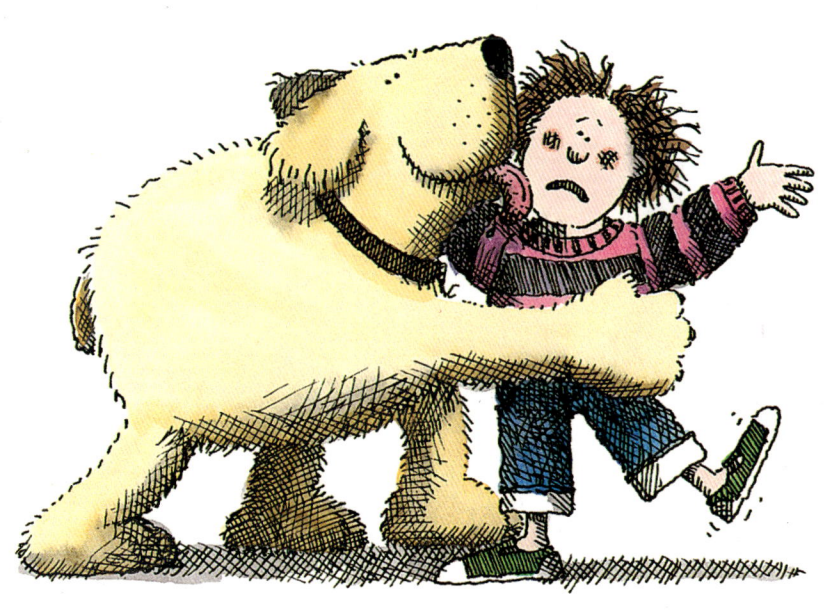

If she gets dirty, I give her a wash.

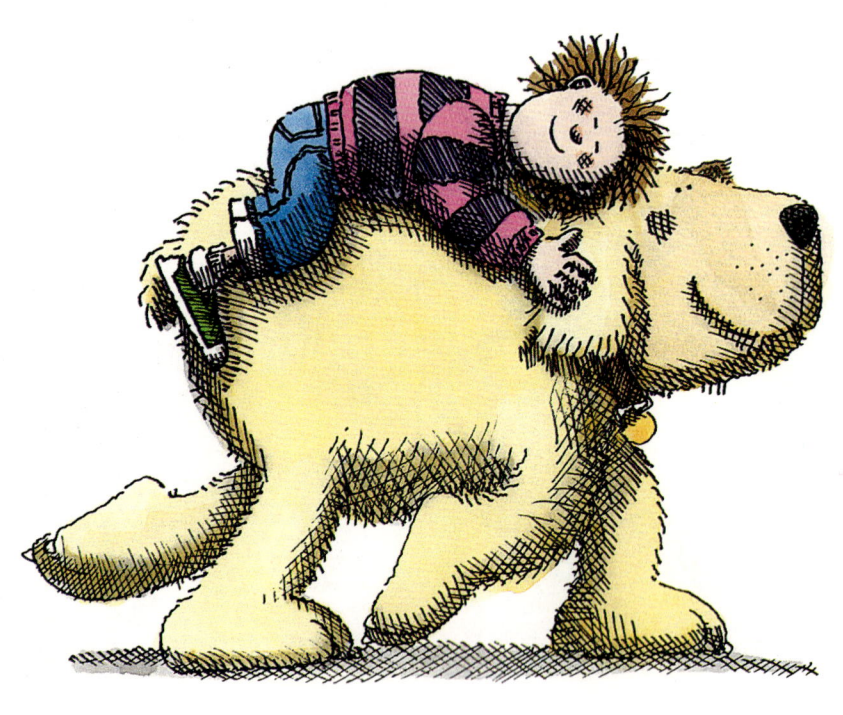

When she's tired, I take her home

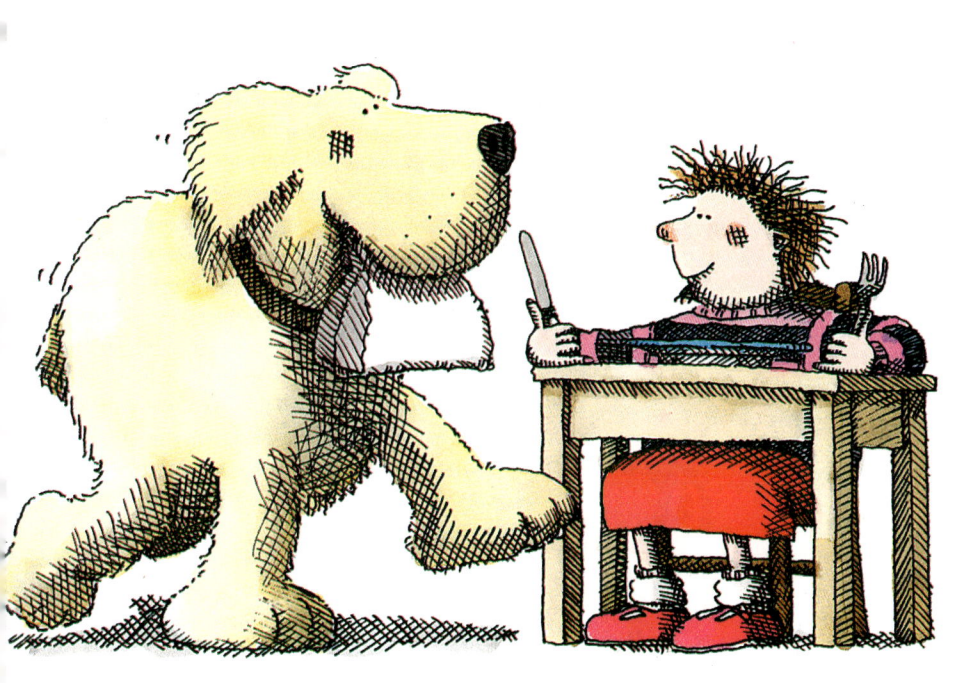

and get her dinner.

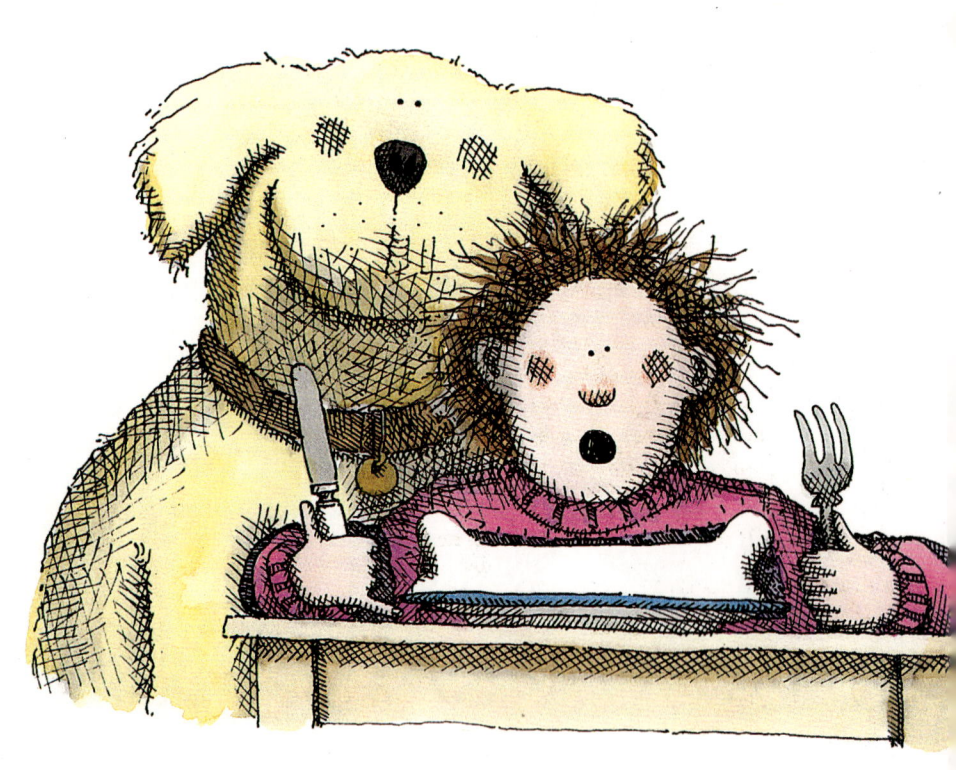

Isn't she lucky?